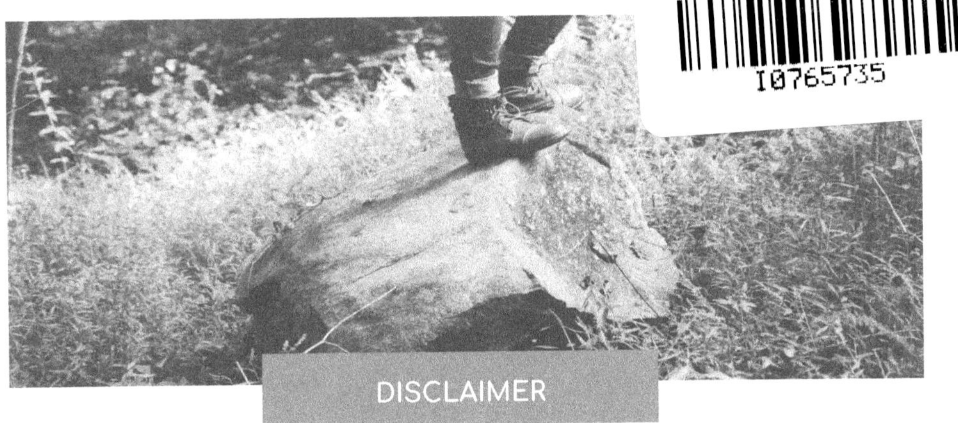

DISCLAIMER

The contents here-in are a compilation of informational material that has assisted me in my understanding and application in making decisions toward my personal safety. In my personal research I made every effort to reference that which was credible and relevant.

In sharing, I make no guarantees, implied or otherwise, that the reader will acquire skills or a perfected state of personal protection by choosing and/or utilizing any methods, tools, training, or advice offered for consideration.

I offer no psychological, financial, legal, or medical advice. Nothing in this writing, on my website, or any other content constitutes a promise or guarantee, implied or otherwise, the user will become skilled and/or achieve limited and/or a perfected state of personal protection.

Personal protection/safety is the sole responsibility of the individual. Individual level of skill is dependent upon multiple factors including experience, basic and trained skill sets, resources, knowledge, discipline, and other factors.
As such factors are individually variable and vary greatly; I cannot and do not offer promise or guarantee any person or person's safety.

Copyright *notice*

Dear reader. This book has been created after many years of experience. Please, be aware, that to share it without author permission is strictly prohibited. The copyright belongs to the author. If you would like to use information from this book, it's allowed only when you use the name of the author or source links. If you have any questions about the rights of sharing this content, do not hesitate to contact me.

I really appreciate your understanding.
With love, Women Aware and Prepared

Thank you

Contents

01.

I get it. You want to know what kind of pepper spray to buy and how to use it. Will it really keep you more safe? And maybe, what are some other ways to stay more safe?

You find yourself concerned for your safety and not wanting to feel helpless and vulnerable. Me too. I have a crazy life story in which I needed to learn this info and learn it FAST. I found a top level self-defense expert and went into learning overdrive over the past 6 years. I've read and researched so much to stay safe and want to help many other women stay safe too.

You've always known that it would be helpful to have some kind of tool for self-protection, especially in these days of uncertainty, BUT you find yourself wondering where to start. Is pepper spray the answer?

If you are someone who doesn't like to feel helpless, this info

may aid you in starting a transformation from a sense of vulnerability to a better sense of preparedness.

I'll be your guide in this ebook to help you through your questions about pepper spray and its use.

I'll save you time as I've gathered all the best info about pepper spray and women's self-defense and have simply and succinctly shared it here in an easy to read format. You can worry less and start doing something about your safety.

In this quick read packed full of helpful tips, I'll help you understand pepper spray and what I have learned about how to select a pepper spray that fits your personal expectations. You may learn some additional things to do to stay more safe and possibly outsmart the bad guy.

Statistics

1 in 3 WOMEN will be attacked with the intent of sexual assault in her lifetime

- 70% of victims of rape know their assailant

- 80% of sexual assault attacks are on women under the age of 30

- More than 50% of rapes occur at or within one mile of the victims' homes*

Because of this, you know you need something to help you be safe and you're looking for the perfect tool to do that. I'll teach you about pepper spray and a few other ideas to empower you.

*National Center on Domestic and Sexual Violence

MY STORY

I was 32 with a 3-year-old on my own. I feared for our lives.

I understand what it's like to feel scared and afraid for your safety. Almost 20 years ago, my world fell apart and I found myself in grave danger. I don't remember which day exactly it was that I knew I needed help...

Was it when I received a call from the FBI asking me about the whereabouts of my former husband I had recently divorced from and whom they had been searching for over the past 6 months?

Or was it when I saw him on the news and learned he was possibly in kahoots with another criminal robbing banks? He had gambling debts. He wasn't well. Due to his constant harrassment of me and his attempt to kidnap our son (whom I had custody of), I knew it was time to become a victor, not a victim, so I could protect myself and son.

What I figured out was that my dad couldn't be with me everywhere I went. The police couldn't show up the instant I needed them. I needed to be able to defend myself and my son. My safety was up to ME.

a person who happens to train law enforcement and intelligence agencies, and who over the past 6 years has trained me how to outsmart the "bad guy." I don't claim to be an expert, and I never wanted to be a "badass." I just wanted to live! In peace! I'll share with you my journey so that you may too claim back your life! Claim back your sanity! It's yours to have. You deserve comfort and peace of mind.

I'll share with you, woman to woman

what I learned in my own transformation from scared and helpless to confident and prepared.

So, I started learning, just like you are right now

lesson by lesson, workshop by workshop. I put one foot in front of the other and began my journey of gaining my peace of mind back - whether it be fear from the specific threat I had looming, or from any criminal intent to harm me.

Congratulations!

for standing up for yourself as you begin your own journey with a next step - learning about one of the many tools to protect yourself: pepper spray!

Let's learn the two things to know before buying pepper spray, but first...

What IS
Pepper Spray?

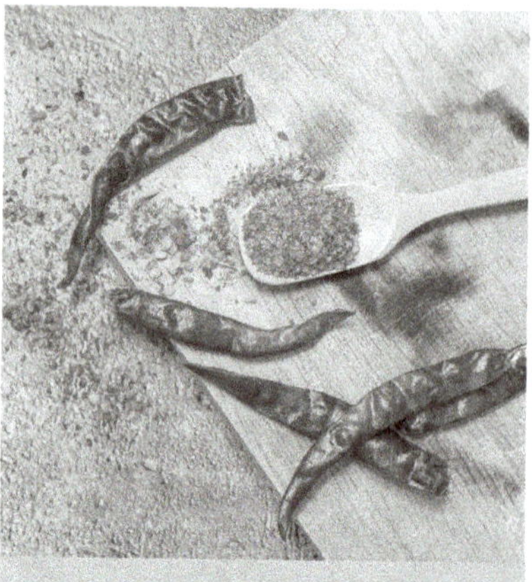

First...

I do realize it may be scary when you start thinking of carrying a "weapon," even if it is non-lethal. You may want to start out with something simple, like pepper spray, but it's very important to understand what it is, how it works, and its limitations.

Pepper spray is an affordable option for a non-lethal self defense product. It mostly consists of Oleoresin Capsicum "OC" (oil that makes up the inflammatory compound in red chili pepper). Pepper spray is eco friendly and all natural.

A small canister of pepper spray is easy to conceal and carry with you in a pocket, backpack or purse.

Pepper spray MAY give you an element of surprise and incapacitate an attacker just long enough to escape a dangerous situation, but depends on many factors.

Is Pepper Spray Legal In My State?

Currently, all 50 states

allow the use of pepper spray WITH RESTRICTIONS for self defense. Some of those states have certain stipulations, though, so make sure to double check your state and local ordinances to note the restrictions listed for you (ex. minimum age, how much you can carry, whether your state allows shipping of pepper spray, etc.).

Remember state restrictions may change, so please look up your own state and read the current restrictions.

On The Federal Level

On the federal level, pepper spray is not allowed in a federal building or in the cabin with you when flying. Checked luggage is usually fine, but double check with your airline before you fly.

Bottom Line

Check your local state and local ordinances for details. You may also call your local police to ask them for details.

06.

The First Thing To Know Before You Buy Pepper Spray

There are different strengths and forms of pepper spray, but the most important aspect of effectiveness is the element of surprise.

If your attacker sees the pepper spray on your keychain or you announce it before you deploy it, he can cover his eyes or possibly grab it from you.

So, let's first set the foundation of pepper spray basics and then we will talk about surprising and outsmarting the bad guy.

Towards the end of this book, I will also recommend the pepper spray I have found that best fits my needs. Then you can decide for yourself which you might choose if you decide to carry pepper spray.

The most important aspect of effectiveness is the element of surprise.

Pepper Spray Basics

What Is The Real Purpose of Pepper Spray?

As in the case of using any self defense tool, the goal is to escape danger. We want to distract and disable an attacker long enough so we may flee to safety.

How Long Has Pepper Spray Been Used?

Pepper spray dates all the way back to ancient military history starting with the Chinese when they burned oil and red pepper and used it against enemy soldiers in 311 B.C. Pepper spray was used in the American Civil War. In 1973, pepper spray was manufactured for personal protection (mainly against dogs). Eventually, law enforcement began replacing their mace with pepper spray ("OC"). Pepper spray became popular for personal safety in the 1990's.

The goal of pepper spray is to give you a moment to escape danger.

What Is Pepper Spray Made Of?

There are 3 different types of chemical irritants

that are classified as non-lethal. Their chemical makeups are different, but the impact on people is similar.

01. "Pepper Spray"

OC is short for oleoresin capsicum and is the oil that is taken from the stem area of a red chili pepper. The OC itself is comprised of several different "capsaicinoids" that are responsible for the strength of OC. Capsaicin is the strongest of them and what is used in most pepper sprays.

02. "Tear Gas"

CS is short for orthochlorobenzalmalonitrile, also known as "tear gas." This is what the first defense sprays contained and is still used in the tear gas models as well as some of the combo sprays. Generally CS has proven to be less effective than OC. It is man made and not eco friendly, whatsoever. It is also suspected of containing carcinogens.

03. "Chemical Mace"

CN is short for alphachloroacetaphenone. It's also called "chemical mace." This is also an older type of defensive spray and has proven, like CS, to be less effective than OC. Like CS, CN is man made and not eco friendly, also suspected of containing carcinogens. Chemical mace was discovered in the 60's.

What Strength of Pepper Spray Should I Buy?

There are three main factors of measuring pepper spray:

1. **OC percentage of oleoresin capsicum** only measures how much chili pepper oil is included.

2. **Scoville Heat Units** (SHU) only measures how spicy the chili pepper is, which is based on a subjective taste test.

SHUs range from 500k to 5.3 million. You will want a rating of at least 1 million SHUs. The concentration determines how long effects will last. Commercial concentrations normally vary from 1 - 20%.

SHU Chart:

 **Bell Peppers** = 0 SHU

 **Jalapenos** = 3,500 SHU

 **Ghost Pepper** = 1,000,000 SHU

 **Pepper Spray** = 2,000,000 SHU

The REAL INDICATOR of heat and potency of your pepper spray is the following: major capsaicinoids.

3. **MC percentage or "major capsaicinoids"** represents the strength of the entire formulation (the SHUs multiplied by the percentage of OC) within the pepper spray. This is the one correct indicator of pepper spray potency, as measured through laboratory testing and recognized by the EPA & US Federal Government.

Typical sprays range from 0.18 to 1.33% MC, with the higher number being the greatest potency. When shopping for pepper spray, PAY ATTENTION to the Major Capsaicinoids (MC) or "Total Capsaicinoids" percentage.

Not All Attackers Respond to pepper spray, especially if intoxicated or mentally ill. When in this state, or with a high tolerance of pain, the person isn't largely affected by the pepper spray.

08.

The Second Thing To Know Before You Buy Pepper Spray

Pepper spray should only be PART of your self defense strategy, not your ONLY self defense strategy.

Please note that pepper spray most likely will NOT immediately stop a determined attacker, especially if he is intoxicated. However, it just may give you that element of surprise and quick second to be able to escape.

The problem is, once you're IN a situation needing to defend yourself, it's difficult to get out unharmed.

A great self defense tool is being aware of your surroundings and noticing a threat when it is present (called "situational awareness").

We want to avoid danger and listen to our intuition. As women, our intuition and our "mama bear" determination are our strengths. Tap into those!

Pepper spray should only be PART of your self defense strategy.

“

The goal is to ESCAPE
danger; to distract and
disable an attacker
long enough to flee.

”

09

Deciding Which Pepper Spray To Carry

There are 3 different spray patterns for pepper spray:

1. Pepper Gel / Stream.....Solid stream, like a squirt gun

PROS
- Greater range. Generally 18 ft.
- Less wind blowback
- Acts quicker
- Sticks to what it hits
- Can target one person out of a group
- Comes out at any angle

CONS
- Fewer bursts per ounce
- Requires greater accuracy to be effective
- Particles may not be inhaled into the respiratory system as well as an aerosol spray

2. Pepper Spray / Mist.....Similar to aerosol hairspray

PROS
- With aerosol nature, greater accuracy
- Most affordable
  Greatest number of bursts/oz.
- Easier to conceal - smaller packaging

CONS
- Can contaminate the environment
- Lack of range
- Most affected by wind blowback and may reach you as well

3. Pepper Foam / Cone....Similar to shaving cream consistency

PROS
- Clings to attacker
- Easy to clean up
- Contaminates less surroundings
- Difficult to remove
- Less need for accuracy

CONS
- Difficult to find for purchase
- Can only reach 10 ft. or so
- Fewer bursts per ounce
- Minimal respiratory effects/ slowest to take effect

Features To Note
when shopping for pepper spray

01.
RANGE

How far can the
pepper spray
reach? How
accurate are you?

02.
CONCENTRATION

The MC
measurement is
around 1.3% for
maximum strength.

03.
EASE OF USE

Consider comfort,
size, accessibility,
and locking
mechanism.

04.
SHELF LIFE

Usually ranges
from 2 - 4 years.
Also depends on
storage and usage.

Some have special features, such as: UV dye ingredient to mark an attacker, LED lights for runners, GPS location alert to loved ones, Loud alarm when deployed, Training videos listed, Comes in a clip, wristbank, keychain, etc. There are larger canisters (ex. 13 oz.) with wall mounts for home defense purposes.

The Kind of Pepper Spray I Carry

I choose to carry Sabre Red Crossfire Pepper Gel for my needs. It is the pepper stream measured at 1.33% MC (maximum strength).

I have the 1.8 oz. canister so it's small enough to conceal but has enough gel to get the job done.

It's rated one of the most effective pepper sprays in multiple outside tests (see Further Resources).

Sabre Red Crossfire can spray 18 bursts up to an 18 ft range with max strength and is the brand trusted by law enforcement.

Its concentrated, powerful stream prevents blowback on you in the wind and has a 4 year shelf life. It is inexpensive, high-quality, lightweight, with a lock, preventing accidental discharge.

I have pepper spray for the purpose of giving me a couple seconds to surprise and incapacitate an attacker just long enough to escape danger.

Where To Purchase

- Amazon with some restrictions such as age and certain states that do not allow shipment of pepper spray.

- Local gun shop or outdoor sporting goods store.

- Prices usually range approximately $12 - $25.

Further Resources
(Look these up:)

- Video comparison of the 3 spray patterns

- Video by SABRE Pepper Gel Advantages

- Top 5 Pepper Sprays of 2020 Article

10.

Effects of Pepper Spray

What Might Happen

OC is an inflammatory agent, which MIGHT cause the attacker to double over. He will have trouble breathing, not enough to be lethal, but it will severely limit his ability and desire to keep attacking, unless in an altered mental state or having a high pain tolerance.

By the way, it may take a second to take effect as the oil has to sink into the membranes of the skin, eyes, nose and mouth.

Results vary depending on the type of pepper spray, the attacker's health, your aim, etc.

It's a good idea to know what to expect so you can anticipate what might happen to an attacker you spray AND what to expect in case some of the pepper spray gets on you.

What To Do If You Get Pepper Spray On You

Pepper sprays, gel and foam are oil based, which makes it most effective. Because oil and water don't mix, water won't remove the pepper spray well unless you use A LOT of it. A baby shampoo that isn't too harsh is best to cleanse the eyes and skin.

Another option to remove pepper spray are decontamination wipes specially designed to wipe spray off skin. Many hospitals and EMT units carry these. You can also find them on Amazon.

If pepper spray gets on you:
• DON'T RUB EYES OR SKIN as that will make the burning feeling worse.
• Don't panic.
• Remove contaminated clothing.
• Wash your skin with soap and water and repeat.
• IF WEARING CONTACTS, throw them away.
• Rinse eyes with water for 15 min. or use baby shampoo which cuts through the oil.

• If you don't have any water with you, blink your eyes continuously.
• Expose skin and eyes to fresh air.
• Get medical attention. Milk is supposed to help skin from burning, but who carries that much milk?

Care and Storage

• Shake pepper spray 1x/mo.
• Test fire quarterly to be sure the nozzle isn't clogged. (Just test with 1 burst using common sense: outdoors, not windy, plenty of open space around you, having soap and water nearby, no bystanders nearby...)
• Replace after expiration date.
• Calendar your test dates and a date to replace it!
• Store in a cool dry area not to exceed temps of 120 degrees F (like a vehicle) or cold temps lower than 32 degrees F. (It may leak or burst and may lose pressure and effective range if not properly stored.)

DO NOT RUB EYES OR SKIN!

11.
Using Pepper Spray

First of all, only use pepper spray if there is ABSOLUTELY no other choice. There are risk factors in using it (getting it on yourself, etc.). Hopefully, you know exactly where that pepper spray is on you so you can grab it quickly and firmly. Ideally, you have practiced with your pepper spray so you are able to unlock and deploy it quickly and easily.

Things To Note

• Practice deploying your pepper spray with each hand. (In case an attacker grabs one of your hands.)
• I'm not aware of any legal requirement to warn an attacker before deploying, but check your state.
• Use your thumb to press the button, giving you a stronger grip than pressing with your index finger.
• Have a backup plan and consider other weapons. Be ready to fight.
• If your pepper spray malfunctions, toss it far away so it cannot be used on you.

As An Attacker Approaches,

• Yell "STAY BACK!" or something similar while you unlock the spray: slide thumb under flip top or twist top to open.
• Stand firmly in an athletic stance: legs shoulder width apart with knees slightly bent.
• Extend your arm far from you and aim at the attacker's face.
• Press the center of the button down with your thumb to fire. (If windy, shield your face as best you can.)
• Spray the attacker's face aiming for the eyes and spraying horizontally from ear to ear.
• Use consistent bursts / sprays. (It takes a second to take full effect so be prepared. He may keep moving towards you.)
• After the eyes are fully sprayed, spray the nose and mouth.
• Move away and escape immediately to call 911.

What If I'm Attacked Anyway?

If an attacker is very sneaky and gets past your situational awareness to surprise you or you find yourself stranded in a dangerous location, be ready by carrying some kind of weapon with you.

NOTE: When women were armed with a knife or gun, only 3% of rape attacks were completed, compared to 32% when the woman was unarmed.

We are all at different levels with what we are comfortable carrying to help protect ourselves. No matter what we carry, we need to be mindful of a few things:

- The tool most likely won't help if you don't know how to use it, haven't practiced with it, and don't carry it with you consistently.
- Always check with your state laws to make sure that what you are carrying is legal.
- Remember there are not-so-obvious tools in everyday life in case you get stuck without carrying a tool (ex: a cup of hot coffee, a pencil, etc.).

PLEASE NOTE: all tools have pros and cons. I share my favorite tools in my online safety course for women and how I layer them in my daily use.

When you're choosing which tool is right for you that best fits your needs and abilities, make a list of the pros and cons of each. Here's an example of pros and cons for pepper spray.

Some basic pros and cons of pepper spray are:

PRO
- Easy to Carry
- Can purchase easily
- Easy to use
- Affordable
- Stand off capability

CON
- It can spray back on you
- It may or may not work

Situational Awareness

If you're aware of your surroundings, you notice a threat before it's a surprise. You are prepared mentally and physically, knowing immediately what to do.

• Become aware of your surroundings
• Listened to your gut feeling
• Made the decision that if you need to, you will fight back
• Trained in self-defense and have something on you to use as a weapon (even a cup of hot coffee!)
• Decided you WILL win!

We want to be smarter, not necessarily stronger. So, we learn how to use our most important safety tool; our minds and intuition.

AVOID denial and listen to your intuition! In my 30 Day Online Safety Course For Women, we go over the different systems to use helping us how to be situationally aware. There are different games you can practice to get used to being aware of your surroundings.

We also learn more about what criminals are looking for in a victim, such as:
• Vulnerability
• Weakness
• Distractions

Be aware of your surroundings and look like you're on a mission. Someone with ill intent may "interview" you by asking a simple question to test if you seem weak or not. For example:
• "Got the time?"
• "Got a light?"

They don't usually choose someone that would put up a fight, so be firm and direct, such as, "I can't help you right now." and keep walking confidently.

Our goal is to learn and practice possible moves (using our tools and even our bodies) so our brain already knows what our muscles need to do automatically when there is a threat. Your fear and your chances of being harmed are decreased because you are prepared and you have options. You've got your power back!

Set Boundaries To Understand Intent

If your words aren't enough to back someone off and you don't have a way to escape safely, you might need to defend yourself physically. Reseach shows that women who fought back did NOT increase their danger. You don't have to be a black belt to fight back! Use a mug of hot coffee, use your elbows, teeth, keys, whatever! Ideally, you have a weapon on you, know exactly where it is and how to use it effectively.

We, as women, are brought up to be nice and polite. If someone isn't listening to your "NO" or "BACK OFF," then get loud and strong! If your voice cannot be loud and strong than buy AND always CARRY a whistle or a "screamer" alarm.

Since we learned that 1 IN 3 WOMEN will be attacked with the intent of sexual assault in her lifetime, and that the majority of attacks are from people we may be familiar with (such as a neighbor, a co-worker...), we now start taking our safety seriously. We arm ourselves with knowledge and preparedness, such as you are doing right now. (Good job!)

Know that a potential attacker will want to keep your interaction friendly. Resist their manipulations. Be rude, be loud! Be sneaky and lie, if needed.

They just crossed a line if they are making you feel uncomfortable and especially if they are not listening to the boundaries you just set. They are no longer a friend. They are an attacker. Treat them like it!

Never plead. Pleading gives an attacker power and control, which fuels the fire for him to continue.

If you have a stranger following you in a dark, empty parking lot and you cannot escape, stop, turn around and face him. Confront him: "I need you to back off!" or "Stop!"

FAQs – Frequently Asked Questions

BEAR SPRAY

What About Bear Spray? Can I Use That?

Bear spray is not manufactured for use against people and is not advised for human to human application.

Consequently, legal issues can arise about injuries and later handicaps that are not legally viable because someone used a product intended for a grizzly against a person. Use of bear spray not out in the wild, shows a sort of indifference, premeditation, and malice so you may want to stay away from this, unless you are hiking outdoors.

The same applies for wasp spray. Use the spray correctly intended for it's purpose.

DOGS

Can I Use Pepper Spray For a Dog Attack?

A dog's nose is more sensitive than a human's nose, so a dog is more susceptible to its effects.

There are pepper sprays made for dog attacks, which have a lower MC percentage than regular pepper spray. Some of those products even have velcro that attaches the spray to your dog leash for easy access.

Be ready to deploy the dog spray as soon as an attacking dog is close enough for the spray to reach it's face. You may want to carry a stick and use that as well. Use your loud voice in addition, if attacked.

12.
Conclusion

As stated in the beginning of this ebook, I'm not an expert. I'm not a badass. I'm just a mom on a mission to stay alive and have a confident assurance that I can defend myself and family.

So, I'm sharing what I've learned for myself from the experts and have found effective.

Remember, the goal is to avoid violence and get to safety.

Sometimes you don't get to choose your circumstances.

Sometimes life gives you lemons and things spin out of control, as I found in my own crazy story. In a matter of a month. Or a week. Or a day. Or even a split second. When you least expect it, of course. You're frozen in fear. What do you do? Is this really happening? Yes, it is. And you have a choice. Act or freeze.

Choose that tool that works for you and know how to fight and win.

Have confidence knowing that one of the most helpful self defense tools is already with you - your mind!

By being situationally aware, using common sense (ex. not parking in a deserted parking garage in a bad part of town at night by yourself) and listening to your intuition, you're already ahead of the game!

We go through a lot more info and practical tips to outsmart an attacker in my online course at WomenAwareAndPrepared. com where I've curated all the best info I've learned from the male dominated world of self-defense and made it a softer place for us women to learn.

What To Do Next

Take the first 3 lessons in my Women's Online Safety
Course for FREE. No strings attached - simply gain more
situational awareness skills in 10-15 minutes. Go to the
website and see the invite at the bottom!

See you there!

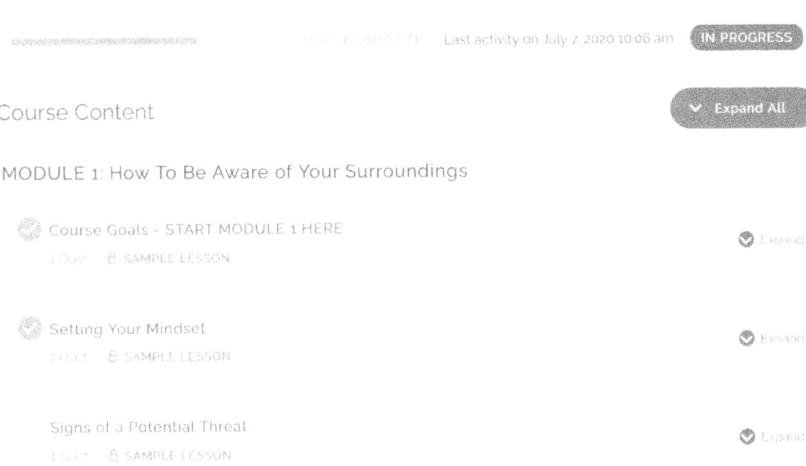

Sample - Women Aware and Prepared

Last activity on July 7, 2020 10:06 am   **IN PROGRESS**

Course Content   **Expand All**

MODULE 1: How To Be Aware of Your Surroundings

Course Goals - START MODULE 1 HERE
SAMPLE LESSON   Expand

Setting Your Mindset
SAMPLE LESSON   Expand

Signs of a Potential Threat
SAMPLE LESSON   Expand

You Don't Have To
Do This Alone!

No more excuses. You're worth keeping safe!

Continue your journey to safety now.

YOU'RE INVITED!

Come on in and join me and a friendly

community of women just like you!

GET YOUR POWER BACK!

www.WomenAwareAndPrepared.com

Sources: WiseWomen / Runnerclick / ActiveResponseTraining
/ ASecureLife / Wikipedia / SafeWise / ModelMugging /
AttackStop / SabreRed